Math Workbook For Kids With Dyscalculia

A resource toolkit book with 100 math activities to overcoming difficulties with numbers

Volume 7

EasyMathGrowth

Introduction

Dyscalculia does not assume that the child does not have the ability to learn mathematics, but rather that a child has a different way of receiving, processing, interpreting mathematical information and therefore it can and should be corrected with adequate stimulation.

Through a specific re-education itinerary that encourages the formation of mental connections, dyscalculia can be overcome.

Dyscalculia must be treated in a very personalized way with each child, making a specific itinerary for each student based on the neuropsychological evaluation that allows knowing what the specific needs of the child are. The intervention by a professional, focuses on a cognitive reeducation itinerary with the aim of stimulating or creating a new neural connection responsible for number concepts and the sense of number. Ways to help your child with math:

1. Use the exercises to strengthen their number sense. These are basic number exercises such as simple operations, quantities and so on. You will find many of these in this book.

2. Use number games. Using games provides a fun sense that favors stimulation and learning.

3. Work with your child or student, basic mathematical concepts such as quantity, proportion (greater, less, much, little ...) and serialization.

4. Lean on visual references that help them understand mathematics (charts, drawings, diagrams ...)

5. Teach your child or student the correspondence between operations and mathematical language (add: union; subtract: remove; multiply: add the same number; divide: distribution)

6. Help them to visualize the problems and to unravel the facts and questions.

7. Train mental math through repeated activities, so as to give the child with dyscalculia cognitive strategies for math.

8. It is very important that you always give the child time to learn and create the relevant neural substrate.

9. Take care of the emotional well-being of the child. It is key that you offer emotional support to avoid derived problems.

10. Adapt the learning process to each child, at their level, their knowledge, their starting needs, etc.

Table of Contents

Addition 1

Addition 2

Addition 3

Addition 4

Addition 5

Addition 6

Addition 7

Addition 8

Addition 9

Subtraction 10

Subtraction 11

Subtraction 12

Subtraction 13

Subtraction 14

Subtraction 15

Subtraction 16

Answer the following questions..17

Write the missing days of the week.................................18

Color the correct answer...19

Solve the following equations...20

Solve the following equations...21

Solve the following equations...22

Solve the following equations...23

Solve the following equations...24

Solve the following equations...25

Solve the following equations...26

Solve the following equations...27

Solve the following equations...28

Table of Contents

Solve the following equations...29

Solve the following equations...30

Solve the following equations...31

Solve the following puzzles..32

Count and select the correct option from the following.............................33

Look at the picture and answer the questions asked below 34

Shapes 35

Shapes 36

Shapes 37

Shapes 38

Shapes 39

Shapes 40

Shapes 41

Shapes 42

Shapes 43

Shapes 44

Shapes 45

Shapes 46

Shapes 47

Shapes 48

Shapes 49

Shapes 50

Shapes 51

Shapes 52

Shapes 53

Shapes 54

Shapes 55

Table of Contents

Solve the following..56

Multiplication..57

Multiplication..58

Multiplication..59

Multiplication..60

Multiplication..61

Multiplication..62

Multiplication..63

Multiplication..64

Multiplication..65

Division..66

Division..67

Division..68

Division..69

Division..70

Division..71

Division..72

Division..73

Division..74

Division..75

Resources..76-125

Addition

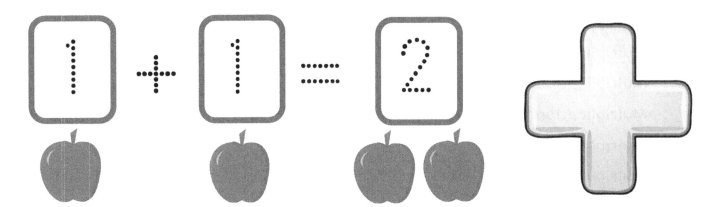

$$1 + 1 = 2$$

Solve the following equations.

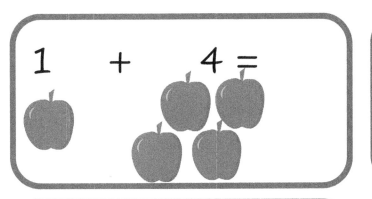

$$1 + 4 =$$

$$1 + 0 =$$

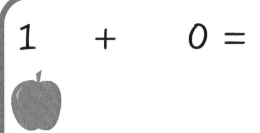

$$1 + 2 =$$

$$1 + 5 =$$

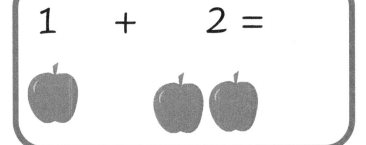

$$1 + 6 =$$

$$1 + 3 =$$

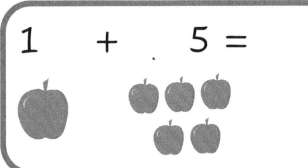

Addition

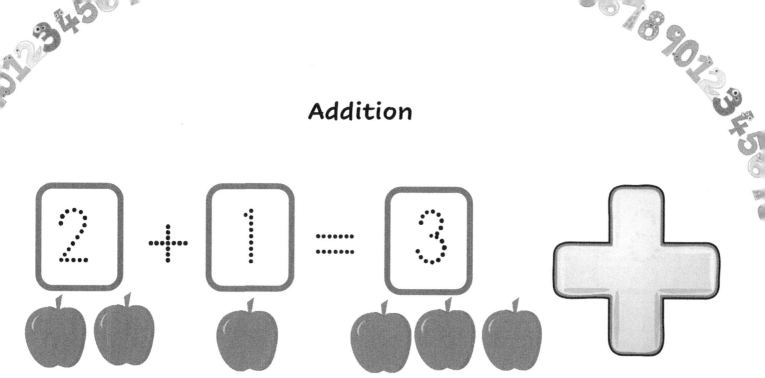

$$2 + 1 = 3$$

Solve the following equations.

$$2 + 2 =$$

$$2 + 4 =$$

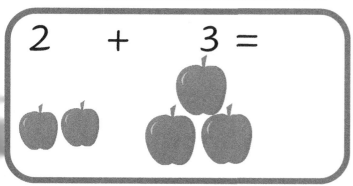

$$2 + 3 =$$

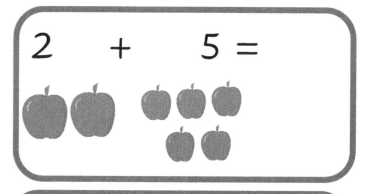

$$2 + 5 =$$

$$2 + 6 =$$

$$2 + 3 =$$

Addition

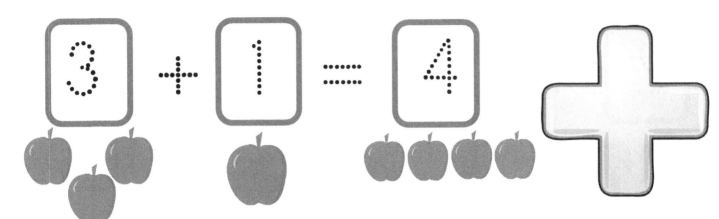

$$3 + 1 = 4$$

Solve the following equations.

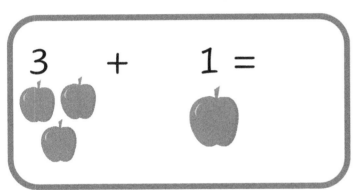

$$3 \quad + \quad 1 =$$

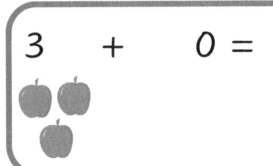

$$3 \quad + \quad 0 =$$

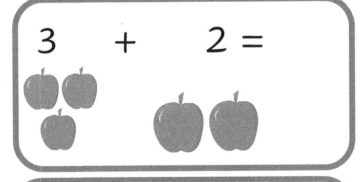

$$3 \quad + \quad 2 =$$

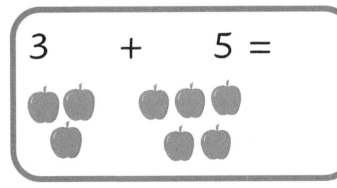

$$3 \quad + \quad 5 =$$

$$3 \quad + \quad 6 =$$

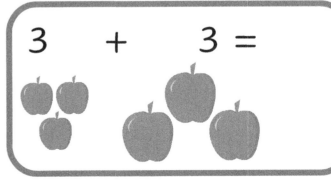

$$3 \quad + \quad 3 =$$

Addition

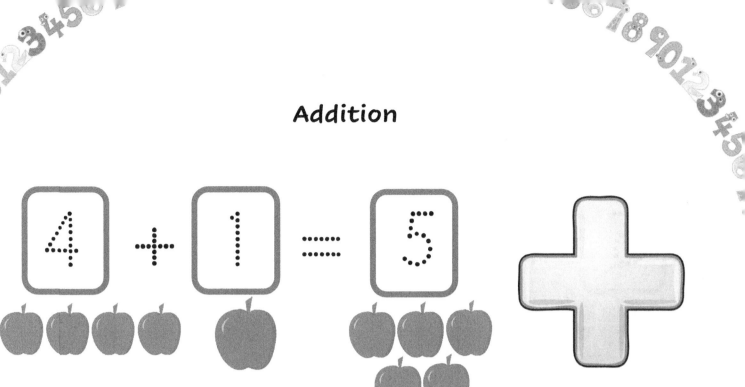

Solve the following equations.

4 + 2 =

4 + 5 =

4 + 3 =

4 + 7 =

4 + 0 =

4 + 9 =

Addition

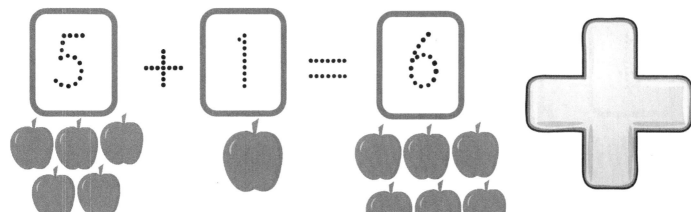

Solve the following equations.

5 + 3 =

5 + 5 =

5 + 2 =

5 + 6 =

5 + 1 =

5 + 7 =

Addition

6 + 1 = 7

Solve the following equations.

6 + 2 =

6 + 5 =

6 + 3 =

6 + 7 =

6 + 0 =

6 + 9 =

Addition

7 + 1 = 8

Solve the following equations.

7 + 1 =

7 + 2 =

7 + 4 =

7 + 0 =

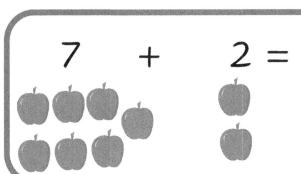

7 + 3 =

7 + 8 =

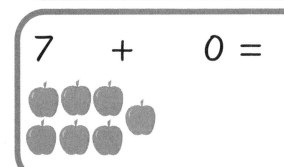

Addition

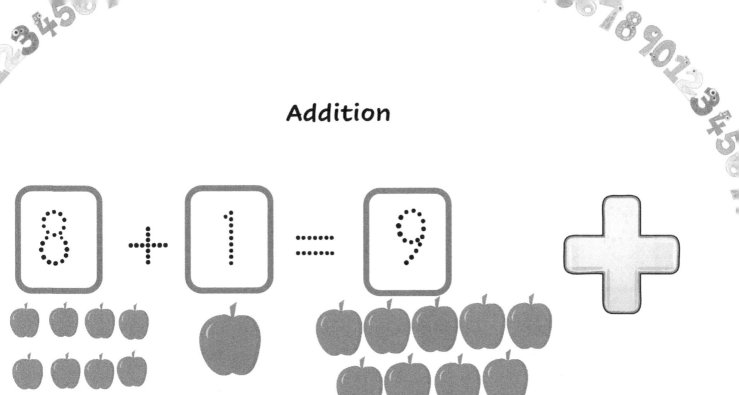

Solve the following equations.

8 + 6 =

8 + 1 =

8 + 2 =

8 + 5 =

8 + 0 =

8 + 8 =

Addition

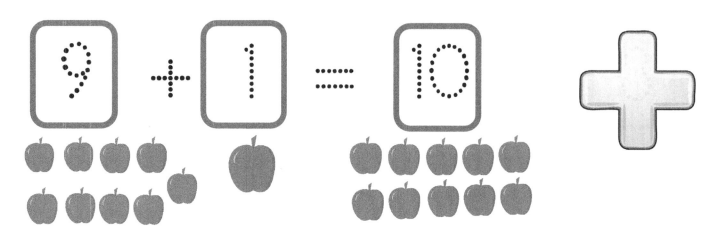

Solve the following equations.

9 + 3 =

9 + 6 =

9 + 4 =

9 + 5 =

9 + 2 =

9 + 7 =

Solve the following equations.

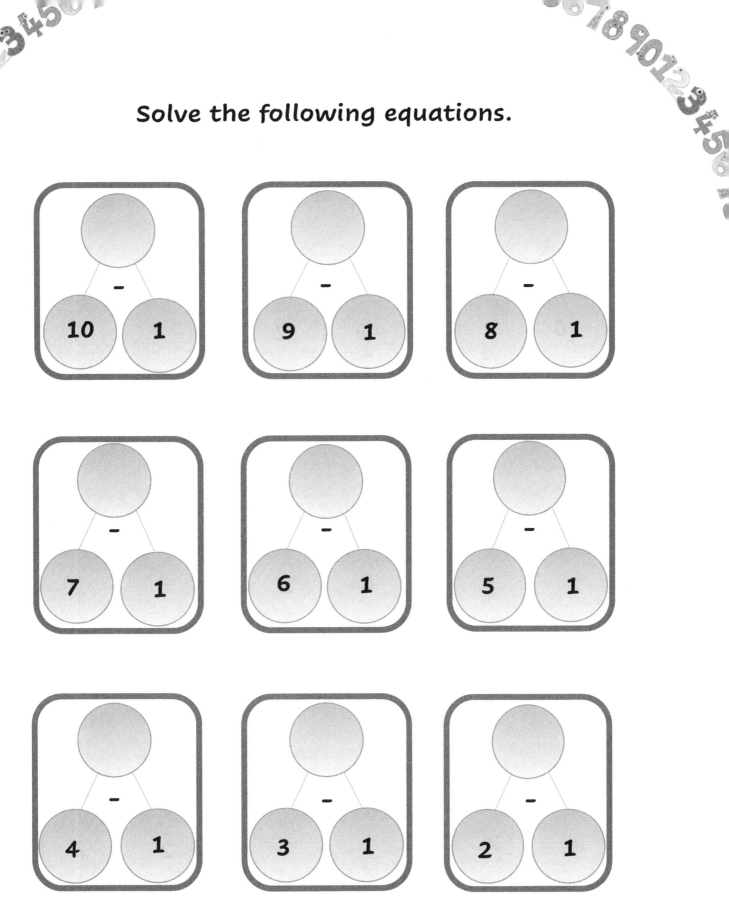

Solve the following equations.

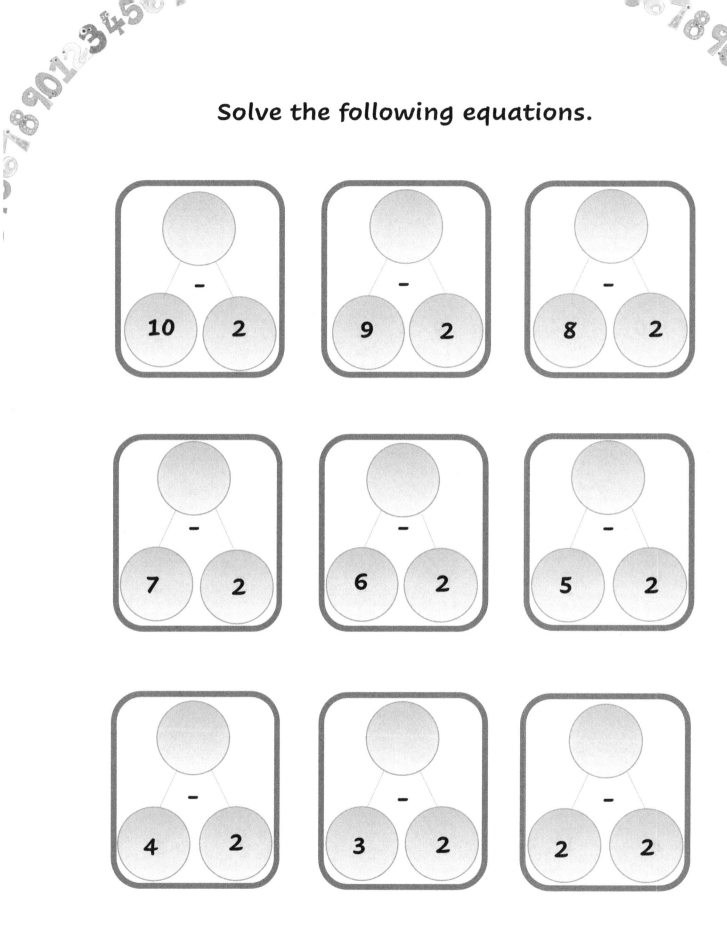

Solve the following equations.

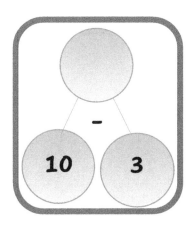

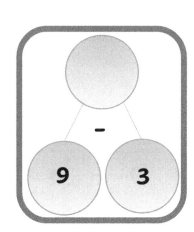

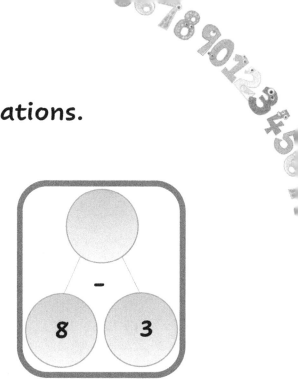

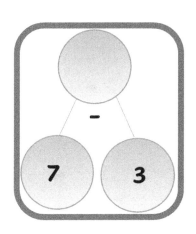

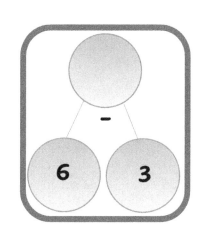

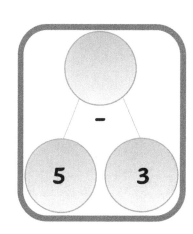

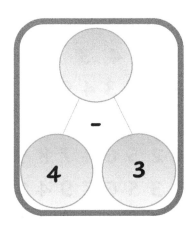

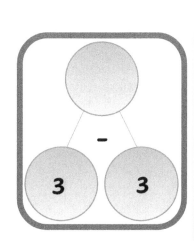

Circle '3'.

1 4 5 3 4 3
6 7 8 3 8 9 3 5
6 7 3 0 5 3 6 4
3 2 5 6 3 7 8 9
3 3 5 6 7 9 0 3
3 5 6 7 3 3 4 5

Solve the following equations.

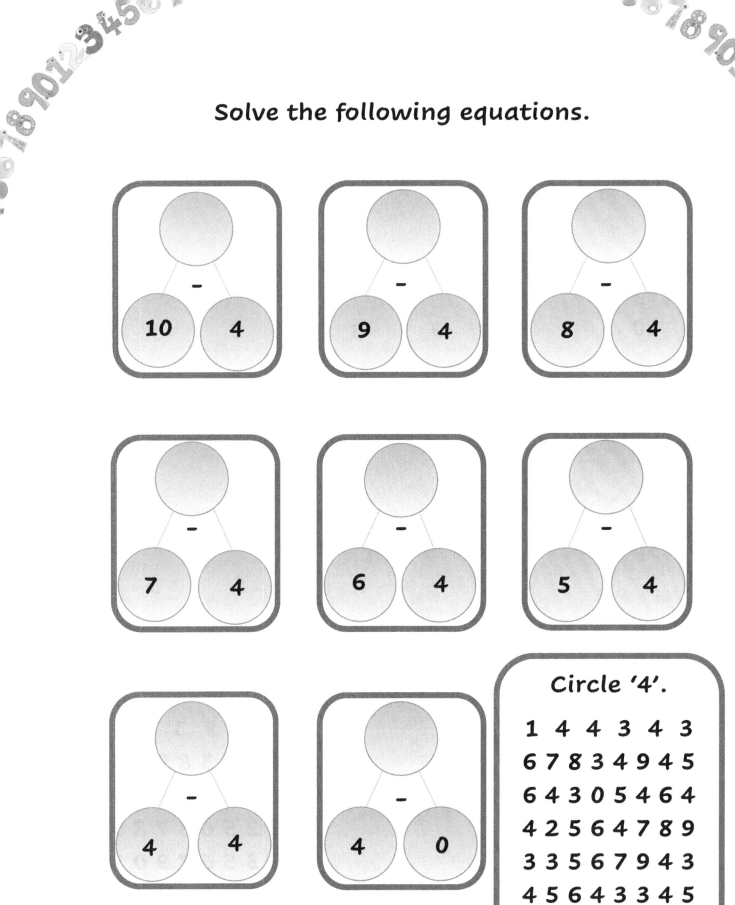

10 − 4

9 − 4

8 − 4

7 − 4

6 − 4

5 − 4

4 − 4

4 − 0

Circle '4'.

1 4 4 3 4 3
6 7 8 3 4 9 4 5
6 4 3 0 5 4 6 4
4 2 5 6 4 7 8 9
3 3 5 6 7 9 4 3
4 5 6 4 3 3 4 5

Solve the following equations.

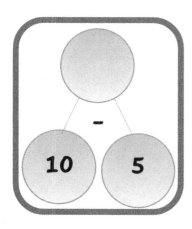

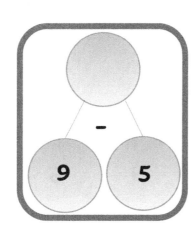

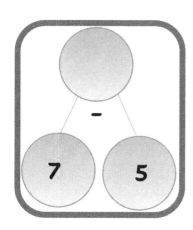

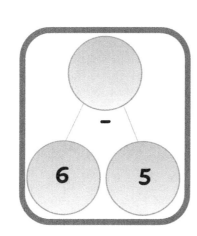

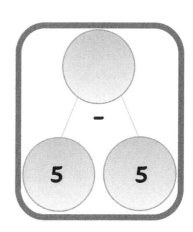

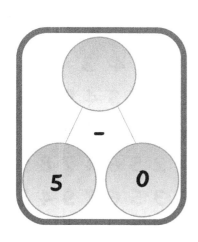

4 5 6 7 4 3 2 1
6 4 4 5 6 7 8 4
How many '4s' are written above?

_____

Circle '4'.

1 4 4 3 4 3
6 7 8 3 4 9 4 5
6 4 3 0 5 4 6 4
4 2 5 6 4 7 8 9
3 3 5 6 7 9 4 3
4 5 6 4 3 3 4 5

Solve the following equations.

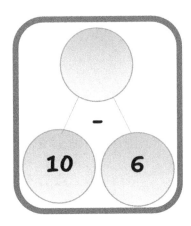

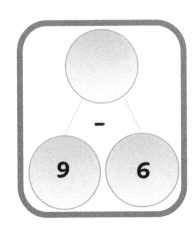

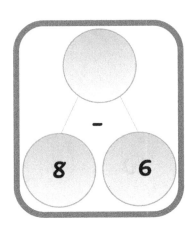

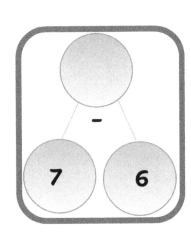

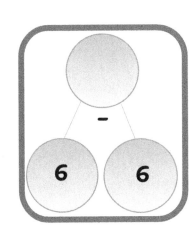

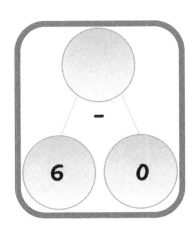

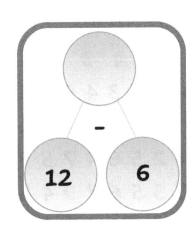

4 5 6 7 4 3 2 1
6 4 4 5 6 7 8 4
How many '6s'
are written
above?

_____

Circle '6'.

1 4 4 3 4 3
6 7 8 3 4 9 4 5
6 4 3 0 5 4 6 4
4 2 5 6 4 7 8 9
3 3 5 6 7 9 4 3
4 5 6 4 3 3 4 5

Solve the following equations.

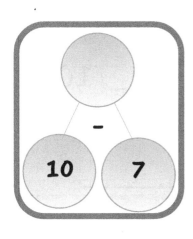 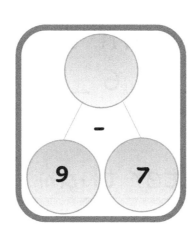 

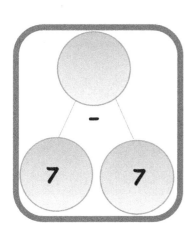 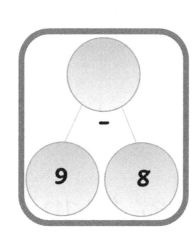 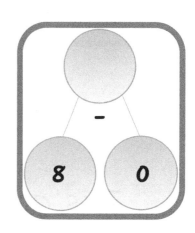

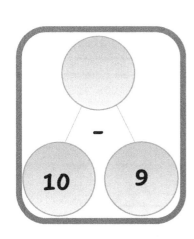

4 8 6 8 4 3 8 8
6 8 4 5 6 8 8 4
How many '8s' are written above?

_____

Circle '7'.

1 7 4 7 4 3
6 7 8 3 7 9 7 5
6 7 3 7 5 7 6 4
4 2 5 7 4 7 7 9
7 3 7 6 7 9 4 7
4 7 6 4 7 3 7 5

Answer the following questions.

Count by 1.
2 ____ ____ 5 6 ____ 8 ____ 10

6 is greater than _____.

2 is smaller than _____.

8 is greater than _____.

7 is greater than _____.

Count by 1.
23 ____ 25 ____ ____ 28 ____ 30

4 is equal to _____.

10 is smaller than _____.

Write the missing days of the week.

Thursday, _____

Monday, _____

_____, Friday

_____, Sunday

Sunday, _____

Monday, _____, Wednesday

Tuesday, _____

Thursday, _____, Saturday

Color the correct answer.

Thirteen is

(13)   (14)   (12)

Twenty is

(12)   (17)   (20)

2 is

(twenty)   (two)   (twelve)

Five is

(Fifty)   (four)   (five)

Forty-two is

(24)   (42)   (244)

Sixty-two is

(92)   (26)   (62)

72 is

(Seventy-two)   (twenty-seven)

twenty-two is

(222)   (22)   (27)

Solve the following equations.

$$4 + 3 =$$

$$3 + 2 =$$

$$7 + 4 =$$

$$8 + 1 =$$

$$6 + 3 =$$

$$9 + 2 =$$

$$7 + 6 =$$

$$6 + 6 =$$

$$5 + 1 =$$

Solve the following equations.

$$4 - 3 = $$

$$3 - 2 = $$

$$7 - 4 = $$

$$8 - 1 = $$

$$6 - 3 = $$

$$9 - 2 = $$

$$7 - 6 = $$

$$6 - 6 = $$

$$5 - 1 = $$

Solve the following equations.

$$22 + 1$$

$$54 + 2$$

$$32 + 1$$

$$11 + 1$$

$$10 + 0$$

$$77 + 2$$

$$77 + 6$$

$$48 + 6$$

$$14 + 1$$

Solve the following equations.

$$\begin{array}{r} 22 \\ +\ 11 \\ \hline \end{array}$$

$$\begin{array}{r} 54 \\ +\ 12 \\ \hline \end{array}$$

$$\begin{array}{r} 32 \\ +\ 11 \\ \hline \end{array}$$

$$\begin{array}{r} 11 \\ +\ 11 \\ \hline \end{array}$$

$$\begin{array}{r} 10 \\ +\ 08 \\ \hline \end{array}$$

$$\begin{array}{r} 77 \\ +\ 22 \\ \hline \end{array}$$

$$\begin{array}{r} 77 \\ +\ 16 \\ \hline \end{array}$$

$$\begin{array}{r} 48 \\ +\ 36 \\ \hline \end{array}$$

$$\begin{array}{r} 14 \\ +\ 31 \\ \hline \end{array}$$

Solve the following equations.

$$22 - 1$$

$$54 - 2$$

$$32 - 1$$

$$11 - 1$$

$$10 - 0$$

$$77 - 2$$

$$77 - 6$$

$$48 - 6$$

$$14 - 1$$

Solve the following equations.

$$\begin{array}{r} 22 \\ -\ 11 \\ \hline \end{array}$$

$$\begin{array}{r} 54 \\ -\ 12 \\ \hline \end{array}$$

$$\begin{array}{r} 32 \\ -\ 11 \\ \hline \end{array}$$

$$\begin{array}{r} 11 \\ -\ 11 \\ \hline \end{array}$$

$$\begin{array}{r} 10 \\ -\ 08 \\ \hline \end{array}$$

$$\begin{array}{r} 77 \\ -\ 22 \\ \hline \end{array}$$

$$\begin{array}{r} 77 \\ -\ 16 \\ \hline \end{array}$$

$$\begin{array}{r} 48 \\ -\ 36 \\ \hline \end{array}$$

$$\begin{array}{r} 14 \\ -\ 31 \\ \hline \end{array}$$

Solve the following equations.

```
  □
+ 3
───
  8
```

```
  □
+ 2
───
  6
```

```
  □
+ 4
────
 10
```

```
  □
+ 6
───
  7
```

```
  □
+ 4
───
  8
```

```
  □
+ 7
────
 11
```

```
  □
+ 9
────
 15
```

```
  □
+ 2
────
 11
```

```
  □
+ 3
───
  4
```

Solve the following equations.

$$\begin{array}{r} -\ 3 \\ \hline 2 \end{array}$$

$$\begin{array}{r} -\ 2 \\ \hline 6 \end{array}$$

$$\begin{array}{r} -\ 4 \\ \hline 0 \end{array}$$

$$\begin{array}{r} -\ 6 \\ \hline 4 \end{array}$$

$$\begin{array}{r} -\ 4 \\ \hline 2 \end{array}$$

$$\begin{array}{r} -\ 7 \\ \hline 1 \end{array}$$

$$\begin{array}{r} -\ 4 \\ \hline 5 \end{array}$$

$$\begin{array}{r} -\ 2 \\ \hline 1 \end{array}$$

$$\begin{array}{r} -\ 3 \\ \hline 6 \end{array}$$

Solve the following equations.

$$\begin{array}{r} \square \\ +\ 13 \\ \hline 88 \end{array}$$

$$\begin{array}{r} \square \\ +\ 12 \\ \hline 16 \end{array}$$

$$\begin{array}{r} \square \\ +\ 24 \\ \hline 40 \end{array}$$

$$\begin{array}{r} \square \\ +\ 66 \\ \hline 77 \end{array}$$

$$\begin{array}{r} \square \\ +\ 24 \\ \hline 48 \end{array}$$

$$\begin{array}{r} \square \\ +\ 27 \\ \hline 81 \end{array}$$

$$\begin{array}{r} \square \\ +\ 09 \\ \hline 55 \end{array}$$

$$\begin{array}{r} \square \\ +\ 62 \\ \hline 91 \end{array}$$

$$\begin{array}{r} \square \\ +\ 63 \\ \hline 84 \end{array}$$

Solve the following equations.

☐	
− 13	
2	

☐	
− 22	
32	

☐	
− 40	
20	

☐	
− 16	
34	

☐	
− 54	
22	

☐	
− 70	
10	

☐	
− 46	
25	

☐	
− 26	
14	

☐	
− 63	
26	

Solve the following equations.

Solve the following equations.

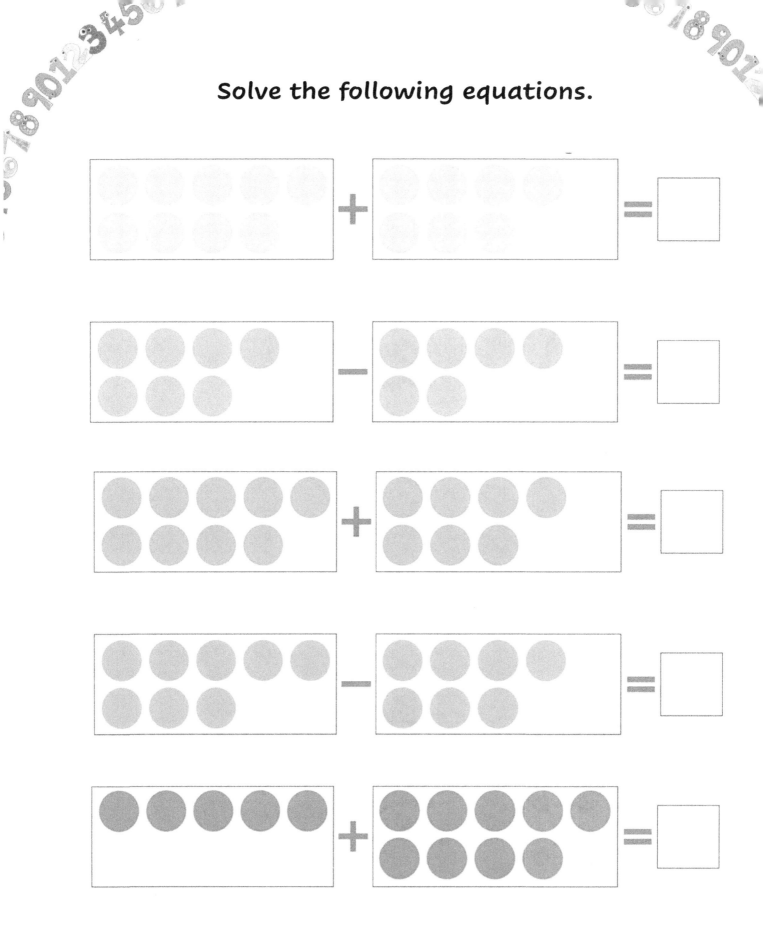

Solve the following puzzles.

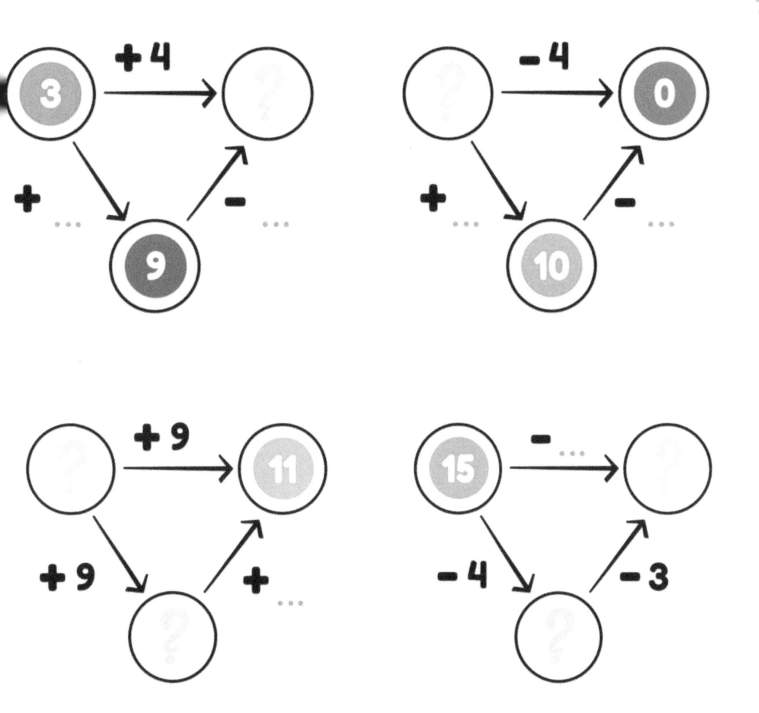

Count and select the correct option from the following.

Look at the picture and answer the questions asked below.

How many Santa clause do you see? _____

How many girls are there? _____

How many Santa clause are not wearing gloves? _____

How many Santa clause have bags? _____

Color, trace and draw the shape below.

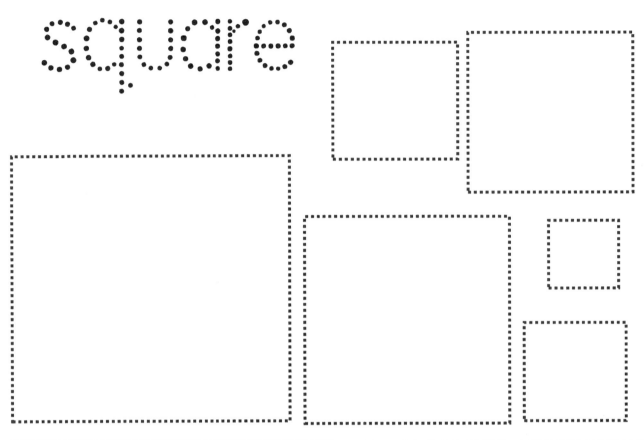

square

| Join the happy faces to draw the shape. | Join the hearts to draw the shape. |

Hello, my name is square,

I have 4 sides and 4 corners

Can you draw hearts on my corners?

Color, trace and draw the shape below.

triangle

Join the happy faces to draw the shape.

Join the hearts to draw the shape.

Hello, my name is triangle,

I have 3 sides and 3 corners.

Can you draw hearts on my corners?

Color, trace and draw the shape below.

Join the happy faces to draw the shape.

Join the hearts to draw the shape.

Hello, my name is circle

I have 0 sides and 0 corners.

Can you draw a circle?

Color, trace and draw the shape below.

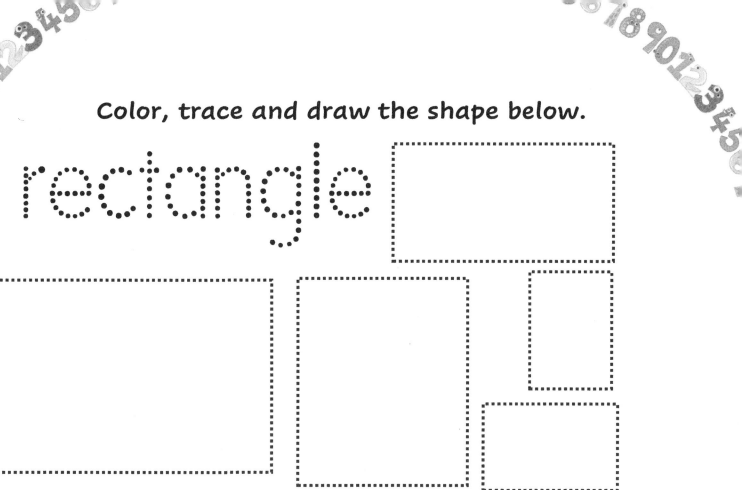

rectangle

Join the happy faces to draw the shape.	Join the hearts to draw the shape.

Hello, my name is rectangle,

I have 4 sides and 4 corners.

Can you draw hearts on my corners?

Color, trace and draw the shape below.

oval

Join the happy faces to draw the shape.

Join the hearts to draw the shape.

Hello, my name is oval,

I have 0 sides and 0 corners.

Can you draw an oval?

Color, trace and draw the shape below.

rhombus

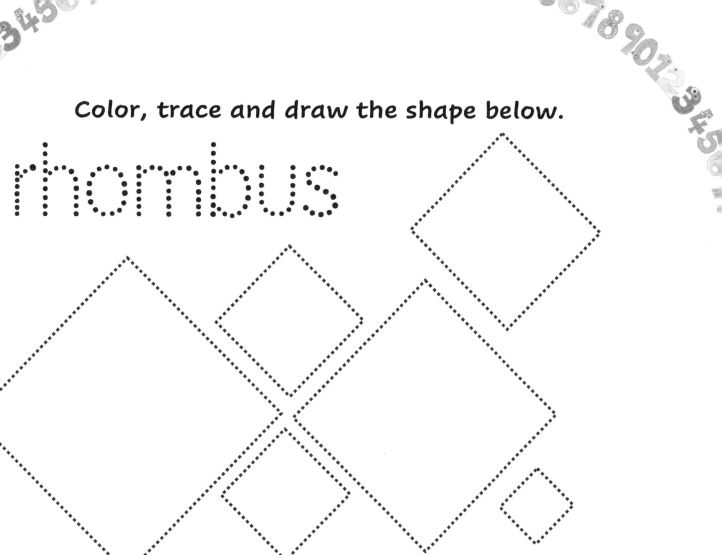

Join the happy faces to draw the shape.

Join the hearts to draw the shape.

Hello, my name is rhombus,

I have 4 sides and 4 corners.

Can you draw hearts on my corners?

Color, trace and draw the shape below.

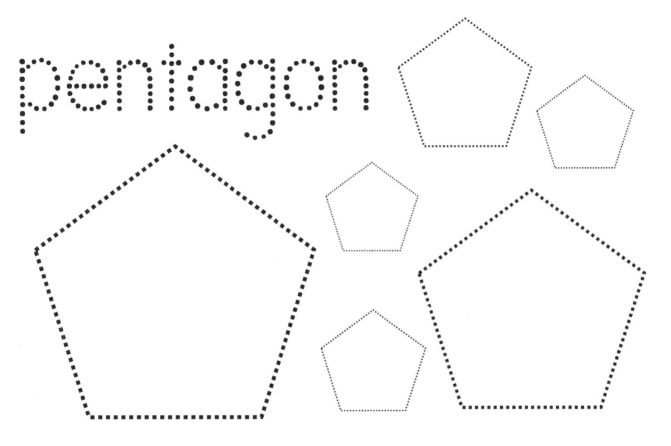

pentagon

Join the happy faces to draw the shape.

Join the hearts to draw the shape.

Hello, my name is pentagon,

I have 5 sides and 5 corners.

Can you draw hearts on my corners?

Color, trace and draw the shape below.

parallelogram

Join the happy faces to draw the shape.

Join the hearts to draw the shape.

Hello, my name is parallelogram,

I have 4 sides and 4 corners.

Can you draw hearts on my corners?

Color, trace and draw the shape below.

hexagon

Join the happy faces to draw the shape.

Join the hearts to draw the shape.

Hello, my name is hexagon,

I have 6 sides and 6 corners.

Can you draw hearts on my corners?

Color, trace and draw the shape below.

heptaagon

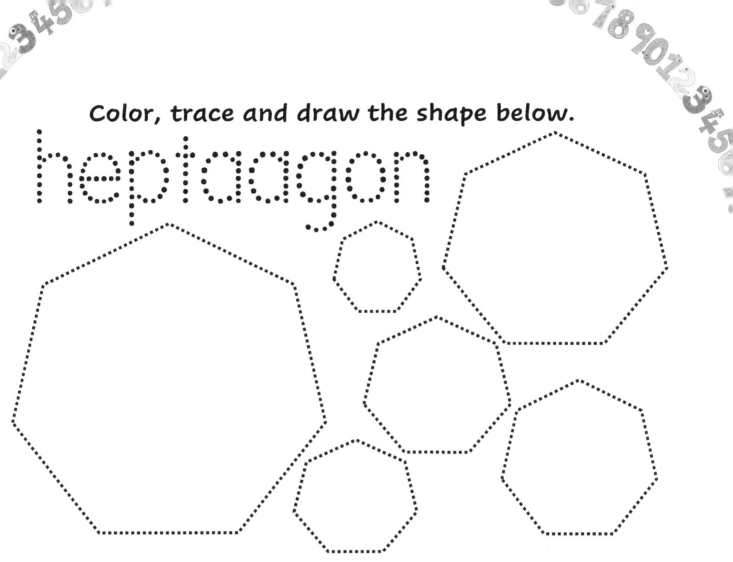

Join the happy faces to draw the shape.

Join the hearts to draw the shape.

Hello, my name is heptagon,

I have 7 sides and 7 corners.

Can you draw hearts on my corners?

Color, trace and draw the shape below.

octagon

Join the happy faces to draw the shape.

Join the hearts to draw the shape.

Hello, my name is octagon,

I have 8 sides and 8 corners.

Can you draw hearts on my corners?

Color, trace and draw the shape below.

nonagon.

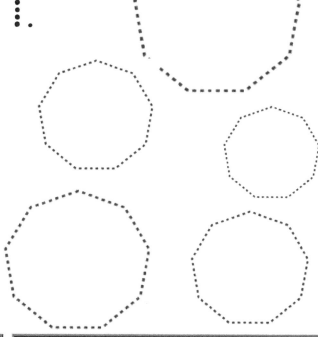

Join the happy faces to draw the shape.	Join the hearts to draw the shape.

Hello, my name is nonagon,

I have 9 sides and 9 corners.

Can you draw hearts on my corners?

Color, trace and draw the shape below.
semicircle

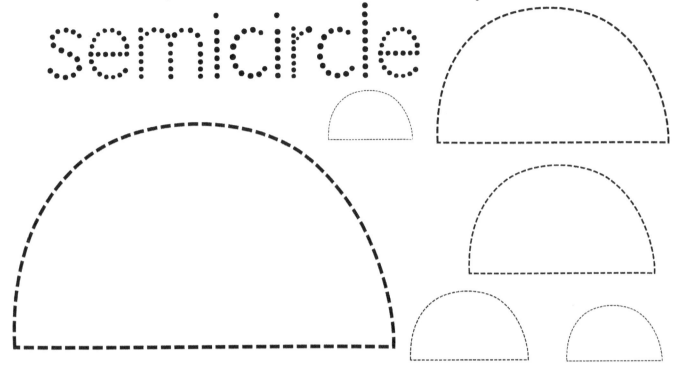

Join the happy faces to draw the shape.

Join the hearts to draw the shape.

Hello, my name is semicircle,

I have 2 sides and 2 corners.

Can you draw hearts on my corners?

Color, trace and draw the shape below.

trapezoid

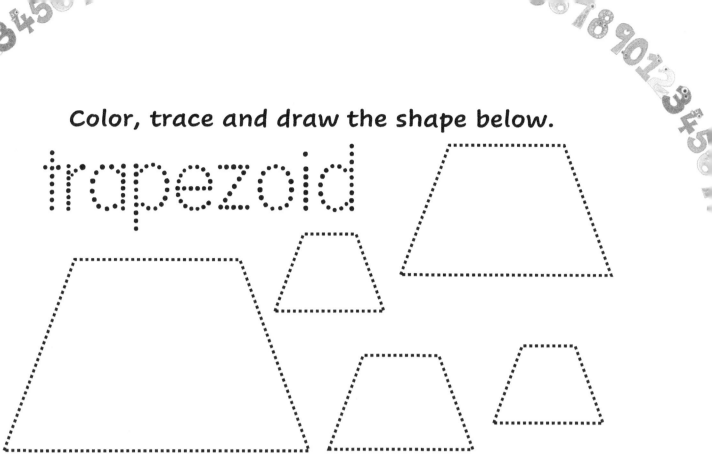

Join the happy faces to draw the shape.

Join the hearts to draw the shape.

Hello, my name is trapezoid,

I have 4 sides and 4 corners.

Can you draw hearts on my corners?

Color, trace and draw the shape below.

sphere

Join the happy faces to draw the shape.

Join the hearts to draw the shape.

Hello, my name is sphere,

Can you draw a sphere?

Color, trace and draw the shape below.

cone

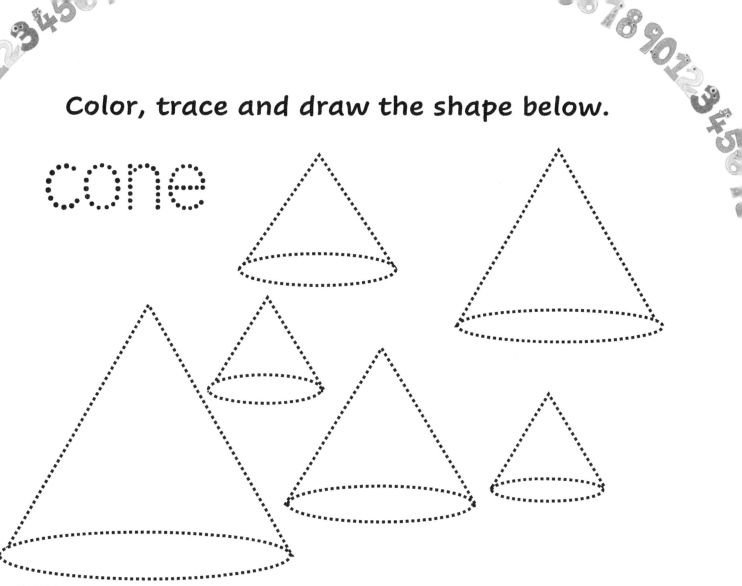

Join the happy faces to draw the shape.

Join the hearts to draw the shape.

Hello, my name is cone,

Can you draw a cone?

Color, trace and draw the shape below.

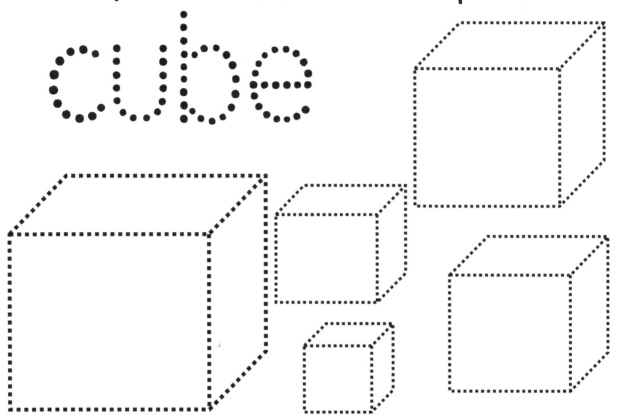

Join the happy faces to draw the shape.

Join the hearts to draw the shape.

Hello, my name is cube,

Can you draw a cube?

Color, trace and draw the shape below.

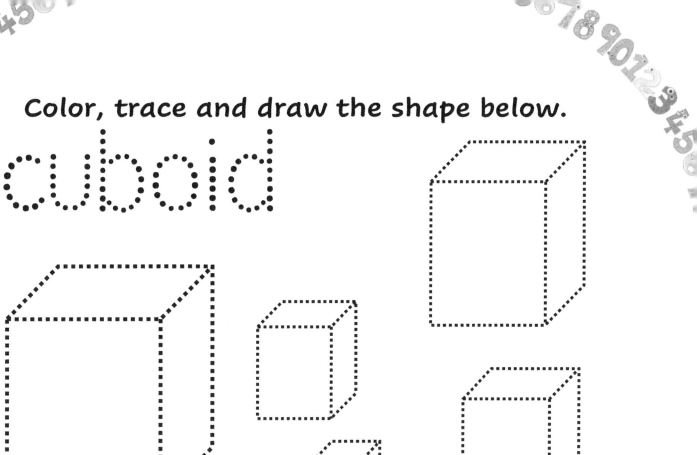

cuboid

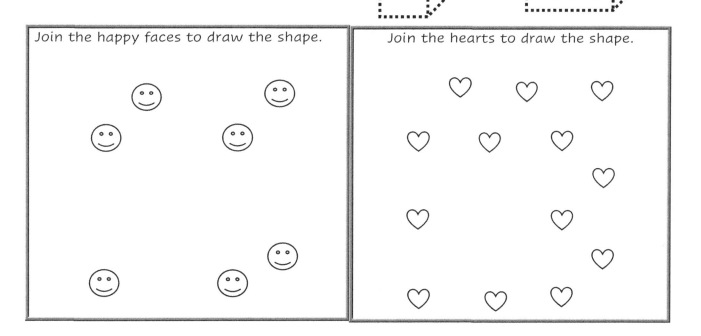

Join the happy faces to draw the shape.

Join the hearts to draw the shape.

Hello, my name is cuboid,

Can you draw a cuboid?

Color, trace and draw the shape below.

pyramid

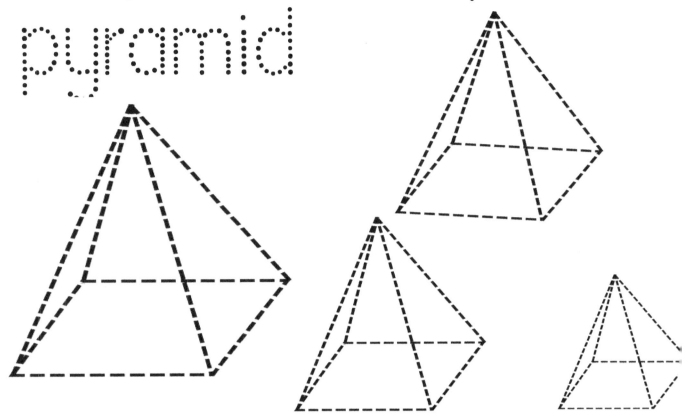

Join the happy faces to draw the shape.

Join the hearts to draw the shape.

Hello, my name is pyramid,

Can you draw a pyramid?

Color, trace and draw the shape below.

prism

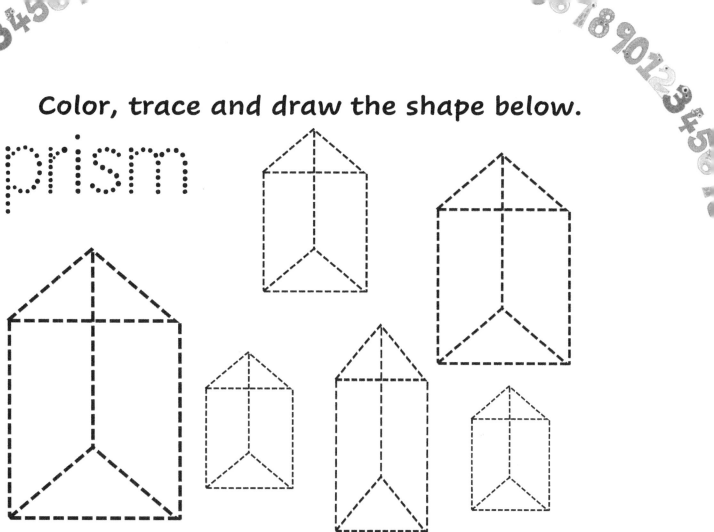

Join the happy faces to draw the shape.

Join the hearts to draw the shape.

Hello, my name is prism,

Can you draw a prism?

Color, trace and draw the shape below.

cylinder

Join the happy faces to draw the shape.	Join the hearts to draw the shape.

Hello, my name is cylinder,

Can you draw a cylinder?

Solve the following.

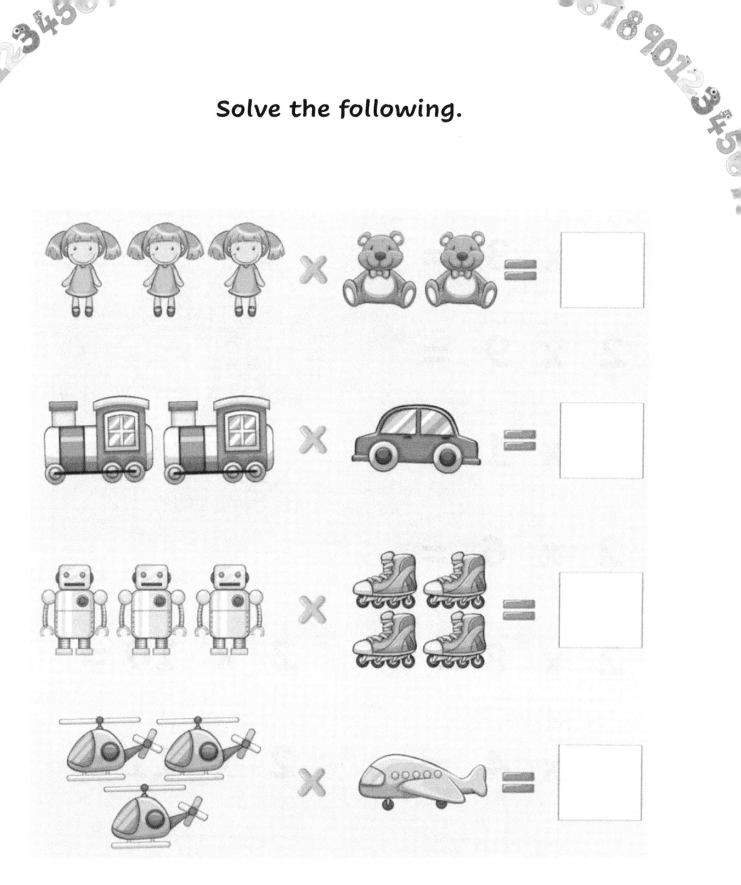

With the help of the multiplication circle solve the following equations.

2 x 3 =

2 x 9 =

2 x 1 =

2 x 6 =

2 x 8 =

2 x 10 =

2 x 4 =

2 x 11 =

2 x 7 =

2 x 2 =

With the help of the multiplication circle solve the following equations.

3 x 3 =

3 x 9 =

3 x 1 =

3 x 6 =

3 x 8 =

3 x 10 =

3 x 4 =

3 x 11 =

3 x 7 =

3 x 5 =

With the help of the multiplication circle solve the following equations.

4 x 3 =

4 x 3 =

4 x 1 =

4 x 6 =

4 x 8 =

4 x 10 =

4 x 4 =

4 x 11 =

4 x 7 =

4 x 5 =

With the help of the multiplication circle solve the following equations.

5 x 3 =

5 x 9 =

5 x 1 =

5 x 6 =

5 x 8 =

5 x 10 =

5 x 4 =

5 x 11 =

5 x 7 =

5 x 2 =

With the help of the multiplication circle solve the following equations.

6 x 3 =

6 x 9 =

6 x 1 =

6 x 6 =

6 x 8 =

6 x 10 =

6 x 4 =

6 x 11 =

6 x 7 =

6 x 2 =

With the help of the multiplication circle solve the following equations.

7 x 3 =

7 x 9 =

7 x 1 =

7 x 6 =

7 x 8 =

7 x 4 =

7 x 7 =

7 x 10 =

7 x 11 =

7 x 2 =

With the help of the multiplication circle solve the following equations.

8 x 3 =

8 x 9 =

8 x 1 =

8 x 6 =

8 x 8 =

8 x 10 =

8 x 4 =

8 x 11 =

8 x 7 =

8 x 2 =

With the help of the multiplication circle solve the following equations.

9 x 3 =

9 x 9 =

9 x 1 =

9 x 6 =

9 x 8 =

9 x 10 =

9 x 4 =

9 x 11 =

9 x 7 =

9 x 2 =

With the help of the multiplication circle solve the following equations.

10 x 3 =

10 x 9 =

10 x 1 =

10 x 6 =

10 x 8 =

10 x 10 =

10 x 4 =

10 x 11 =

10 x 7 =

10 x 2 =

65

With the help of the division table solve the following equations.

1 ÷ 1 =

2 ÷ 1 =

3 ÷ 1 =

4 ÷ 1 =

÷ 1
1 ÷ 1 = 1
2 ÷ 1 = 2
3 ÷ 1 = 3
4 ÷ 1 = 4
5 ÷ 1 = 5
6 ÷ 1 = 6
7 ÷ 1 = 7
8 ÷ 1 = 8
9 ÷ 1 = 9
10 ÷ 1 = 10
11 ÷ 1 = 11
12 ÷ 1 = 12

5 ÷ 1 =

8 ÷ 1 =

6 ÷ 1 =

9 ÷ 1 =

7 ÷ 1 =

10 ÷ 1 =

With the help of the division table solve the following equations.

$2 \div 2 =$

$4 \div 2 =$

$6 \div 2 =$

$8 \div 2 =$

$\div$ 2		
$2 \div 2 =$		1
$4 \div 2 =$		2
$6 \div 2 =$		3
$8 \div 2 =$		4
$10 \div 2 =$		5
$12 \div 2 =$		6
$14 \div 2 =$		7
$16 \div 2 =$		8
$18 \div 2 =$		9
$20 \div 2 =$		10
$22 \div 2 =$		11
$24 \div 2 =$		12

$10 \div 2 =$

$16 \div 2 =$

$12 \div 2 =$

$18 \div 2 =$

$14 \div 2 =$

$20 \div 2 =$

With the help of the division table solve
the following equations.

$$3 \div 3 =$$

$$6 \div 3 =$$

$$9 \div 3 =$$

$$12 \div 3 =$$

÷ 3			
3 ÷	3	=	1
6 ÷	3	=	2
9 ÷	3	=	3
12 ÷	3	=	4
15 ÷	3	=	5
18 ÷	3	=	6
21 ÷	3	=	7
24 ÷	3	=	8
27 ÷	3	=	9
30 ÷	3	=	10
33 ÷	3	=	11
36 ÷	3	=	12

$$15 \div 3 =$$

$$24 \div 3 =$$

$$18 \div 3 =$$

$$27 \div 3 =$$

$$21 \div 3 =$$

$$30 \div 3 =$$

With the help of the division table solve the following equations.

$$4 \div 4 =$$

$$8 \div 4 =$$

$$12 \div 4 =$$

$$16 \div 4 =$$

$\div$	4		
4	$\div$	4	= 1
8	$\div$	4	= 2
12	$\div$	4	= 3
16	$\div$	4	= 4
20	$\div$	4	= 5
24	$\div$	4	= 6
28	$\div$	4	= 7
32	$\div$	4	= 8
36	$\div$	4	= 9
40	$\div$	4	= 10
44	$\div$	4	= 11
48	$\div$	4	= 12

$$20 \div 4 =$$

$$32 \div 4 =$$

$$24 \div 4 =$$

$$36 \div 4 =$$

$$28 \div 4 =$$

$$40 \div 4 =$$

With the help of the division table solve the following equations.

$$5 \div 5 =$$

$$10 \div 5 =$$

$$15 \div 5 =$$

$$20 \div 5 =$$

÷ 5			
5	÷ 5	=	1
10	÷ 5	=	2
15	÷ 5	=	3
20	÷ 5	=	4
25	÷ 5	=	5
30	÷ 5	=	6
35	÷ 5	=	7
40	÷ 5	=	8
45	÷ 5	=	9
50	÷ 5	=	10
55	÷ 5	=	11
60	÷ 5	=	12

$$25 \div 5 =$$

$$40 \div 5 =$$

$$30 \div 5 =$$

$$45 \div 5 =$$

$$35 \div 5 =$$

$$50 \div 5 =$$

With the help of the division table solve the following equations.

$$6 \div 6 =$$

$$12 \div 6 =$$

$$18 \div 6 =$$

$$24 \div 6 =$$

$$30 \div 6 =$$

$$36 \div 6 =$$

$$42 \div 6 =$$

$$48 \div 6 =$$

$$54 \div 6 =$$

$$60 \div 6 =$$

$\div$ 6			
6	$\div$ 6	=	1
12	$\div$ 6	=	2
18	$\div$ 6	=	3
24	$\div$ 6	=	4
30	$\div$ 6	=	5
36	$\div$ 6	=	6
42	$\div$ 6	=	7
48	$\div$ 6	=	8
54	$\div$ 6	=	9
60	$\div$ 6	=	10
66	$\div$ 6	=	11
72	$\div$ 6	=	12

With the help of the division table solve the following equations.

$$7 \div 7 =$$

$$14 \div 7 =$$

$$21 \div 7 =$$

$$28 \div 7 =$$

$\div$ 7		
7 $\div$ 7	=	1
14 $\div$ 7	=	2
21 $\div$ 7	=	3
28 $\div$ 7	=	4
35 $\div$ 7	=	5
42 $\div$ 7	=	6
49 $\div$ 7	=	7
56 $\div$ 7	=	8
63 $\div$ 7	=	9
70 $\div$ 7	=	10
77 $\div$ 7	=	11
84 $\div$ 7	=	12

$$35 \div 7 =$$

$$56 \div 7 =$$

$$42 \div 7 =$$

$$63 \div 7 =$$

$$49 \div 7 =$$

$$70 \div 7 =$$

With the help of the division table solve the following equations.

÷ 8

8	÷	8	=	1
16	÷	8	=	2
24	÷	8	=	3
32	÷	8	=	4
40	÷	8	=	5
48	÷	8	=	6
56	÷	8	=	7
64	÷	8	=	8
72	÷	8	=	9
80	÷	8	=	10
88	÷	8	=	11
96	÷	8	=	12

$8 \div 8 =$

$16 \div 8 =$

$24 \div 8 =$

$32 \div 8 =$

$40 \div 8 =$

$64 \div 8 =$

$48 \div 8 =$

$72 \div 8 =$

$56 \div 8 =$

$80 \div 8 =$

With the help of the division table solve the following equations.

$9 \div 9 =$

$18 \div 9 =$

$27 \div 9 =$

$36 \div 9 =$

$\div$	**9**
$9 \div 9 = 1$	
$18 \div 9 = 2$	
$27 \div 9 = 3$	
$36 \div 9 = 4$	
$45 \div 9 = 5$	
$54 \div 9 = 6$	
$63 \div 9 = 7$	
$72 \div 9 = 8$	
$81 \div 9 = 9$	
$90 \div 9 = 10$	
$99 \div 9 = 11$	
$108 \div 9 = 12$	

$45 \div 9 =$

$72 \div 9 =$

$54 \div 9 =$

$81 \div 9 =$

$63 \div 9 =$

$90 \div 9 =$

With the help of the division table solve the following equations.

$$10 \div 10 =$$

$$20 \div 10 =$$

$$30 \div 10 =$$

$$40 \div 10 =$$

$\div$ 10		
$10 \div 10 = 1$		
$20 \div 10 = 2$		
$30 \div 10 = 3$		
$40 \div 10 = 4$		
$50 \div 10 = 5$		
$60 \div 10 = 6$		
$70 \div 10 = 7$		
$80 \div 10 = 8$		
$90 \div 10 = 9$		
$100 \div 10 = 10$		
$110 \div 10 = 11$		
$120 \div 10 = 12$		

$$50 \div 10 =$$

$$80 \div 10 =$$

$$60 \div 10 =$$

$$90 \div 10 =$$

$$70 \div 10 =$$

$$100 \div 10 =$$

Resources: Cut, Laminate and use as a resource.

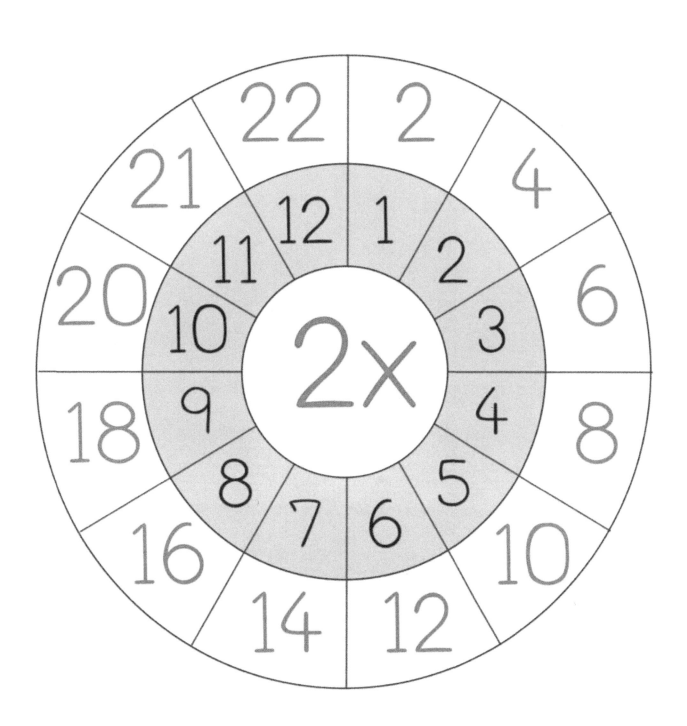

This page is intentionally left blank.

Resources: Cut, Laminate and use as a resource.

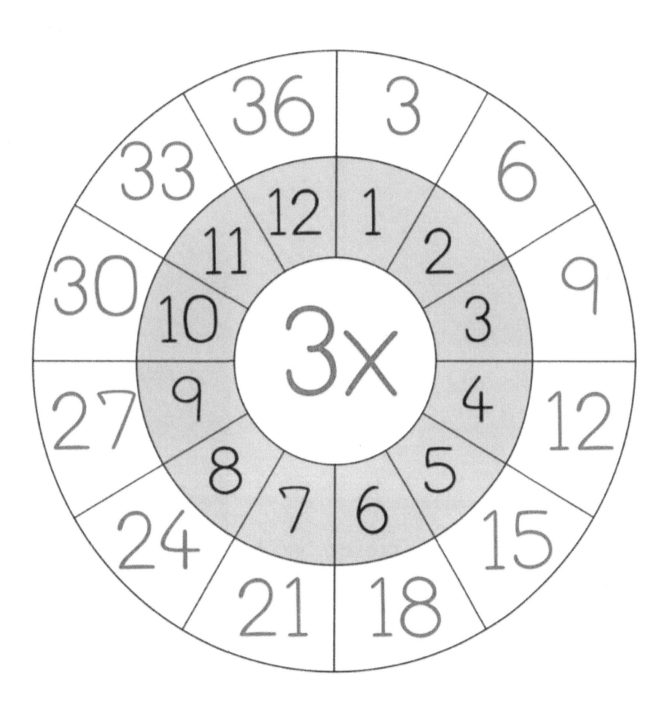

This page is intentionally left blank.

Resources: Cut, Laminate and use as a resource.

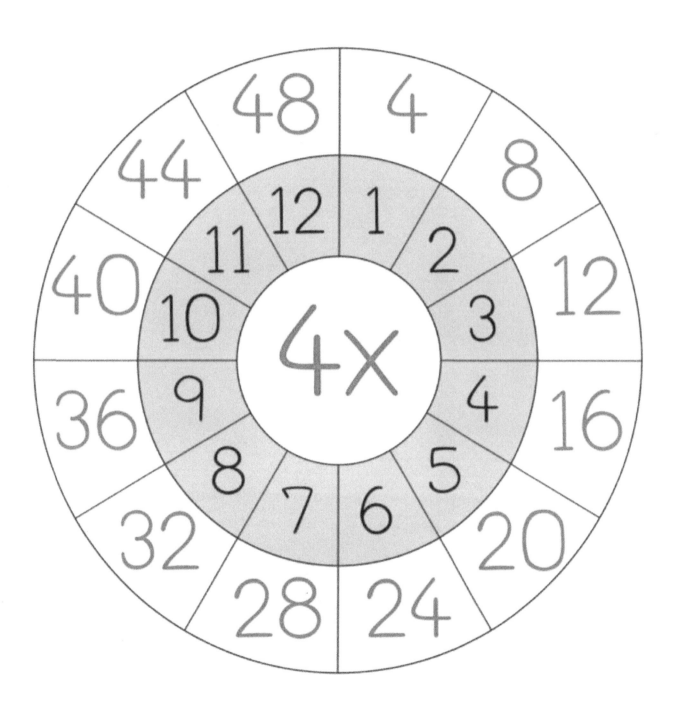

This page is intentionally left blank.

Resources: Cut, Laminate and use as a resource.

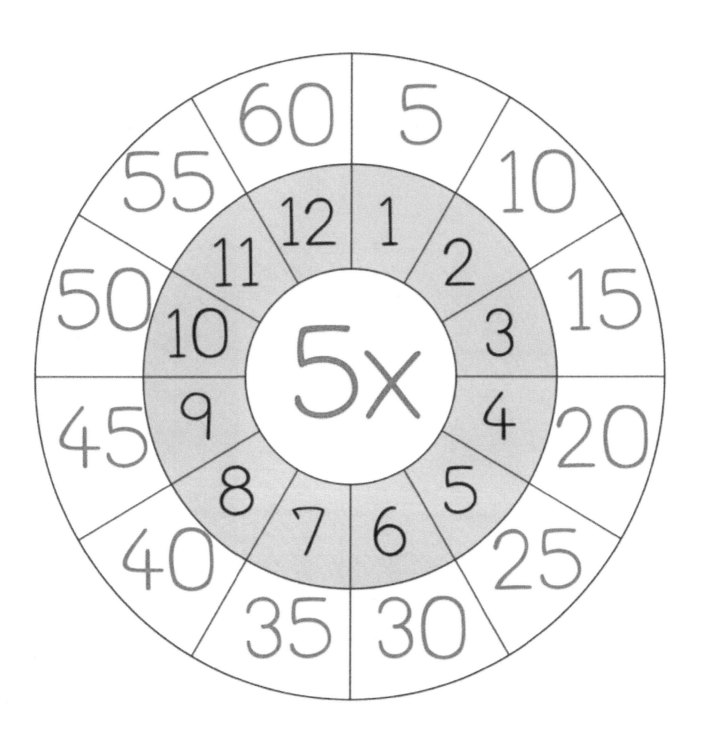

This page is intentionally left blank.

Resources: Cut, Laminate and use as a resource.

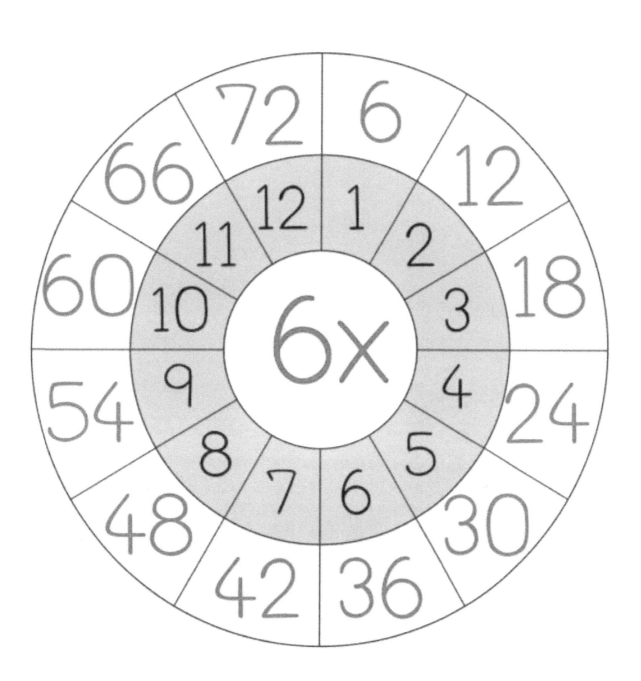

This page is intentionally left blank.

Resources: Cut, Laminate and use as a resource.

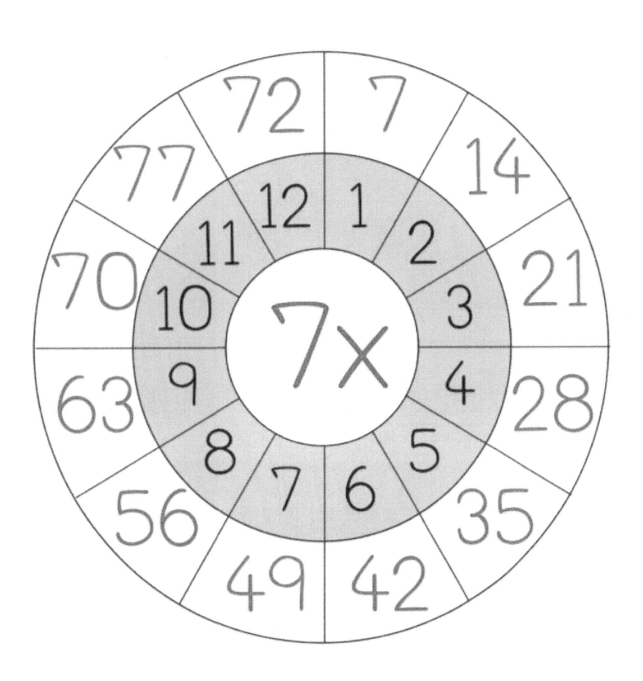

This page is intentionally left blank.

Resources: Cut, Laminate and use as a resource.

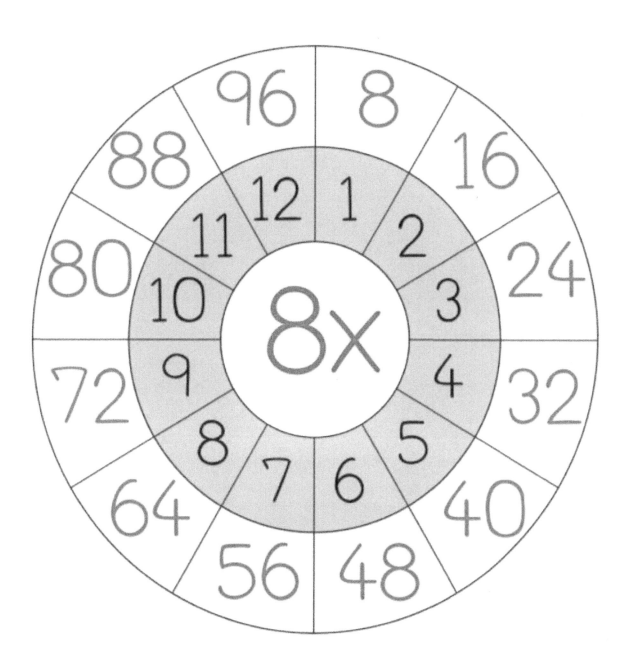

This page is intentionally left blank.

Resources: Cut, Laminate and use as a resource.

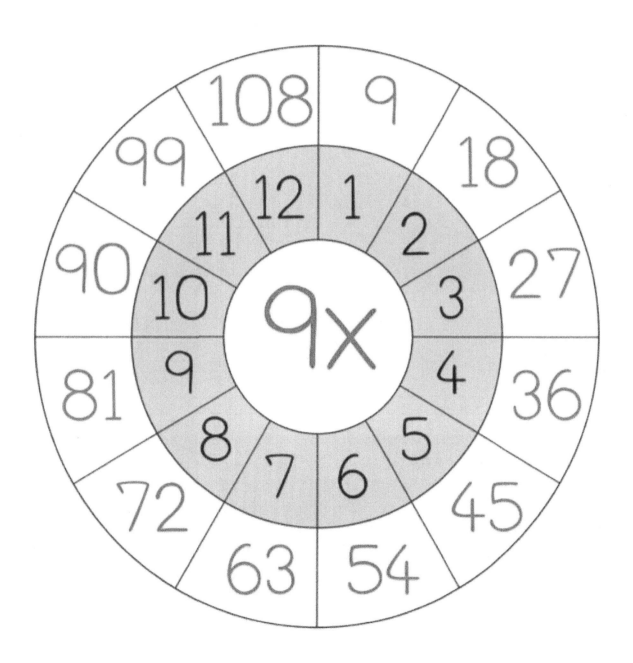

This page is intentionally left blank.

Resources: Cut, Laminate and use as a resource.

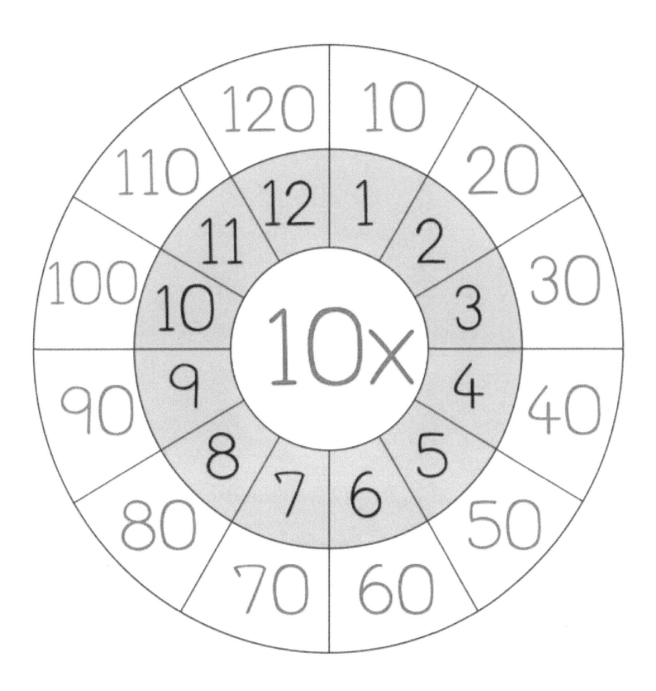

This page is intentionally left blank.

Resources: Cut, Laminate and use as a resource.

÷ 1

1	÷	1	=	1
2	÷	1	=	2
3	÷	1	=	3
4	÷	1	=	4
5	÷	1	=	5
6	÷	1	=	6
7	÷	1	=	7
8	÷	1	=	8
9	÷	1	=	9
10	÷	1	=	10
11	÷	1	=	11
12	÷	1	=	12

This page is intentionally left blank.

Resources: Cut, Laminate and use as a resource.

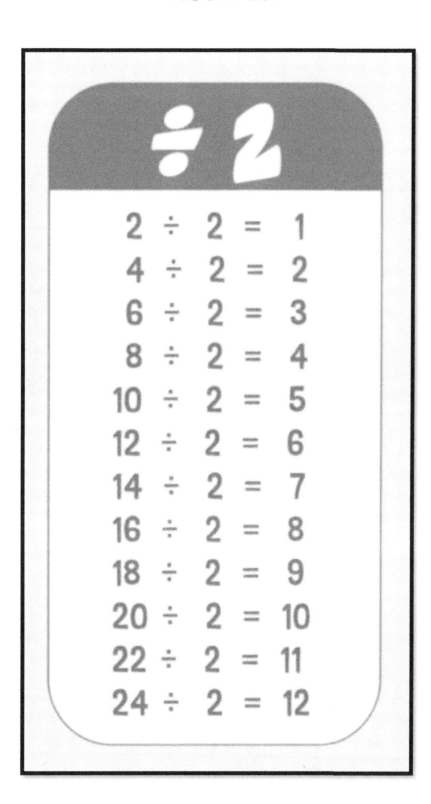

$$2 \div 2 = 1$$
$$4 \div 2 = 2$$
$$6 \div 2 = 3$$
$$8 \div 2 = 4$$
$$10 \div 2 = 5$$
$$12 \div 2 = 6$$
$$14 \div 2 = 7$$
$$16 \div 2 = 8$$
$$18 \div 2 = 9$$
$$20 \div 2 = 10$$
$$22 \div 2 = 11$$
$$24 \div 2 = 12$$

This page is intentionally left blank.

Resources: Cut, Laminate and use as a resource.

÷ 3

3 ÷	3	=	1
6 ÷	3	=	2
9 ÷	3	=	3
12 ÷	3	=	4
15 ÷	3	=	5
18 ÷	3	=	6
21 ÷	3	=	7
24 ÷	3	=	8
27 ÷	3	=	9
30 ÷	3	=	10
33 ÷	3	=	11
36 ÷	3	=	12

This page is intentionally left blank.

Resources: Cut, Laminate and use as a resource.

$$4 \div 4 = 1$$
$$8 \div 4 = 2$$
$$12 \div 4 = 3$$
$$16 \div 4 = 4$$
$$20 \div 4 = 5$$
$$24 \div 4 = 6$$
$$28 \div 4 = 7$$
$$32 \div 4 = 8$$
$$36 \div 4 = 9$$
$$40 \div 4 = 10$$
$$44 \div 4 = 11$$
$$48 \div 4 = 12$$

This page is intentionally left blank.

Resources: Cut, Laminate and use as a resource.

÷ 5

5	÷ 5	=	1
10	÷ 5	=	2
15	÷ 5	=	3
20	÷ 5	=	4
25	÷ 5	=	5
30	÷ 5	=	6
35	÷ 5	=	7
40	÷ 5	=	8
45	÷ 5	=	9
50	÷ 5	=	10
55	÷ 5	=	11
60	÷ 5	=	12

This page is intentionally left blank.

Resources: Cut, Laminate and use as a resource.

÷ 6

$6 \div 6 = 1$

$12 \div 6 = 2$

$18 \div 6 = 3$

$24 \div 6 = 4$

$30 \div 6 = 5$

$36 \div 6 = 6$

$42 \div 6 = 7$

$48 \div 6 = 8$

$54 \div 6 = 9$

$60 \div 6 = 10$

$66 \div 6 = 11$

$72 \div 6 = 12$

This page is intentionally left blank.

Resources: Cut, Laminate and use as a resource.

÷ 7

7	÷ 7	=	1
14	÷ 7	=	2
21	÷ 7	=	3
28	÷ 7	=	4
35	÷ 7	=	5
42	÷ 7	=	6
49	÷ 7	=	7
56	÷ 7	=	8
63	÷ 7	=	9
70	÷ 7	=	10
77	÷ 7	=	11
84	÷ 7	=	12

This page is intentionally left blank.

Resources: Cut, Laminate and use as a resource.

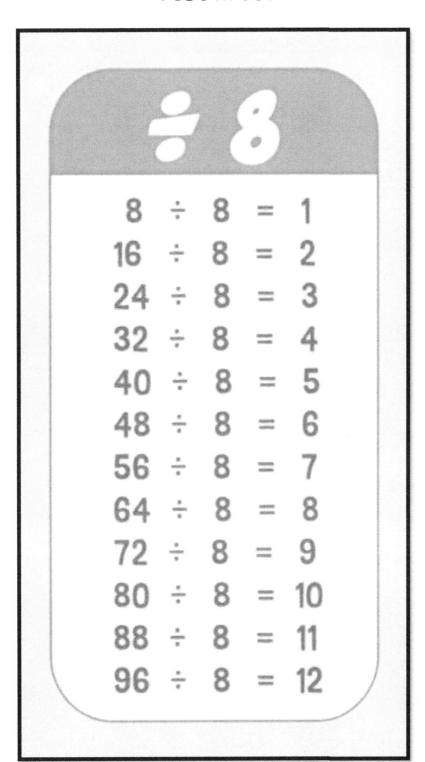

$8 \div 8 = 1$

$16 \div 8 = 2$

$24 \div 8 = 3$

$32 \div 8 = 4$

$40 \div 8 = 5$

$48 \div 8 = 6$

$56 \div 8 = 7$

$64 \div 8 = 8$

$72 \div 8 = 9$

$80 \div 8 = 10$

$88 \div 8 = 11$

$96 \div 8 = 12$

This page is intentionally left blank.

Resources: Cut, Laminate and use as a resource.

9 ÷	9 =	1
18 ÷	9 =	2
27 ÷	9 =	3
36 ÷	9 =	4
45 ÷	9 =	5
54 ÷	9 =	6
63 ÷	9 =	7
72 ÷	9 =	8
81 ÷	9 =	9
90 ÷	9 =	10
99 ÷	9 =	11
108 ÷	9 =	12

$$9 \div 9 = 1$$
$$18 \div 9 = 2$$
$$27 \div 9 = 3$$
$$36 \div 9 = 4$$
$$45 \div 9 = 5$$
$$54 \div 9 = 6$$
$$63 \div 9 = 7$$
$$72 \div 9 = 8$$
$$81 \div 9 = 9$$
$$90 \div 9 = 10$$
$$99 \div 9 = 11$$
$$108 \div 9 = 12$$

This page is intentionally left blank.

Resources: Cut, Laminate and use as a resource.

÷ 10

10	÷ 10	=	1
20	÷ 10	=	2
30	÷ 10	=	3
40	÷ 10	=	4
50	÷ 10	=	5
60	÷ 10	=	6
70	÷ 10	=	7
80	÷ 10	=	8
90	÷ 10	=	9
100	÷ 10	=	10
110	÷ 10	=	11
120	÷ 10	=	12

This page is intentionally left blank.

Resources: Cut, Laminate and use as a resource.
Count and write the number of cupcakes.

This page is intentionally left blank.

Resources: Cut, Laminate and use as a resource. Find the number '9' and '6'.

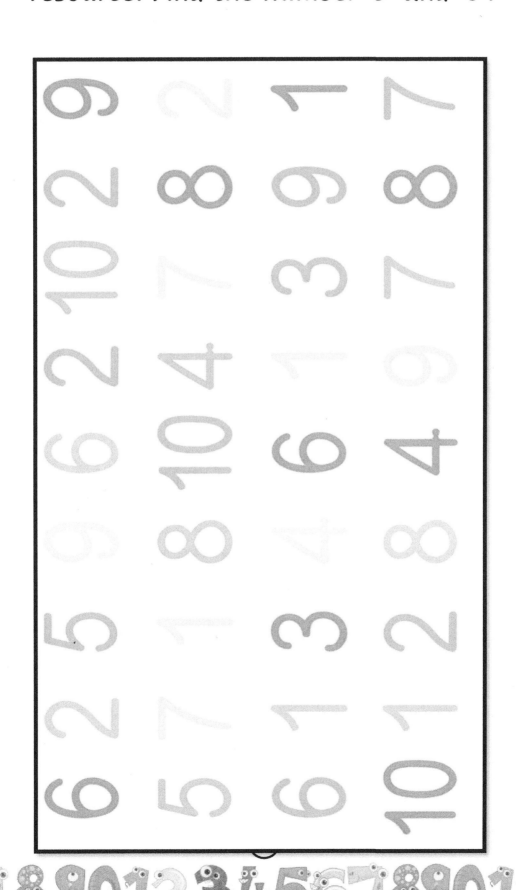

This page is intentionally left blank.

Resources: Cut, Laminate and use as a resource. Solve the equations.

$6-4$

$9-2$

$8+2$

$1+8$

$8-3$

$4-3$

$2+7$

$1+1$

$2+5$

$9+1$

$7-5$

$3+3$

$6-2$

$3+6$

This page is intentionally left blank.

Resources: Cut, Laminate and use as a resource. Find and color the number, '9'.

This page is intentionally left blank.

Resources: Cut, Laminate and use as a resource.

Find the number

Color the cell with the number 5 to receive a picture.

This page is intentionally left blank.

Find the number

Color the cell with the number 6 to receive a picture.

1 9 8
8 6 6
6 6 5
3 5 6 6 8
6
6 3 9 5
9 8
6 6 6 6 1
9 6 3
8 6 5 6
6
9 6
3 9
5 1 8

This page is intentionally left blank.

Made in the USA
Las Vegas, NV
04 December 2024